First Edition Collectible

Geniune Autographed Manuscript

This book was written in one day on **December 13, 2018**. This book is updated every year.

SILLY LITTLE BOYS

Gift Card

Date:

To:

From:

Message:

What Do Books Do?

BOOKS ARE POWERFUL!

Books Educate!
Books Enlighten!
Books Empower!
Books Entertain!
Books Emancipate!
Books Spring Eternal!
Books Drive Exploration!
Books Spark Evolution!
Books Ignite Revolution!

Sharon Esther Lampert
Poet, Philosopher, Prophet, Peacemaker, Prodigy

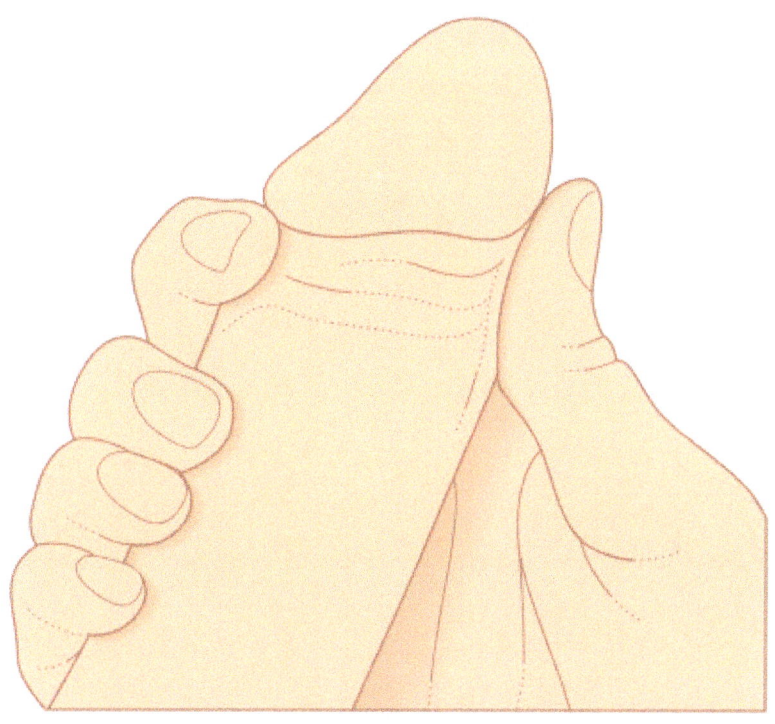

SILLY LITTLE BOYS
40 RULES of MANHOOD

How Do Silly Little Boys Grow Into Sane Big Men

www.SillyLittleBoys.com

#vaginapower #sillylittleboys

Self-Help, Psychology, Relationships, Sex, Literature

SILLY LITTLE BOYS: 40 RULES OF MANHOOD
How Do Silly Little Boys Grow into Sane Big Men   www.SillyLittleBoys.com

#VaginaPower

©January 1st, 2019 by Creative Genius Sharon Esther Lampert. All Rights Reserved.
No part of this book may be used or reproduced in any manner whatsoever without written permission except in the case of brief quotations embodied in critical articles and reviews.

Hardcover   ISBN: 978-1-885872-29-6
Paperback   ISBN: 978-1-885872-35-7
E-Book   ISBN: 978-1-885872-41-8
Library of Congress Catalog Card Number: PCN 2019900006

KADIMAH PRESS: GIFTS OF CREATIVE GENIUS
Books may be purchased for education, business, or sales promotional use.
www.SharonEstherLampert.com

FAN MAIL:
FANS@SharonEstherLampert.com

SillyLittleBoys.com

To order book: INGRAM, 1 Ingram Blvd. La Vergne, TN 37086-3629,
Phone: 615-793-5000

Author and Book Designer: Creative Genius Sharon Esther Lampert

Editor: Dave Segal

Gratitude: Count Your Blessings!
• Love of My Lifetime: Mommy Eve Lampert
• Loves of My Life: Schmaltzy and Falafel www.schmaltzy.com
• Sister Spirit: Hannah Senesh
• MUSE: Kark Bardosh
• MENTOR: Lauren Raiken

First Edition

Manufactured in the United States of America

Creative Genius Sharon Esther Lampert

SILLY LITTLE BOYS
40 RULES of MANHOOD

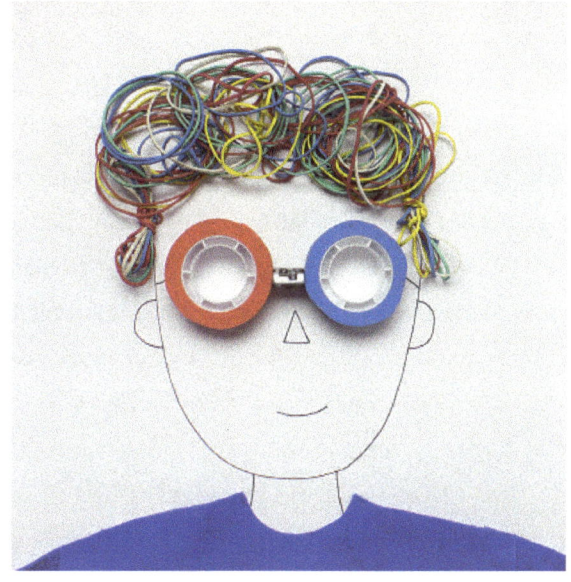

How Do Silly Little Boys Grow Into Sane Big Men

Self Help for Men of All Ages

SILLY LITTLE BOYS: 40 RULES OF MANHOOD

14 Global Catastrophes Because Men Can't Control a Penis

#PENIS WALL OF SHAME

The Rise and Fall from Power for Non-Consensual Sex

Good Boy-Bad Boy Sexual Predators:

Jailbird Jean-Claude Arnault. #2018NOBELPRIZELITERATURE

Jailbird Owen Labrie Lost a 4-Year Scholarship to Harvard Divinity School #BelieveChessyProut15

Pussy Grabber President Donald John Trump #FREEMELANIA

Alleged Supreme Court Justice Brett #BLACKOUT Kavanaugh #BelieveDrFord

Impeached Sex Addict President William Jefferson Clinton #FREEHILLARY

"LUV GOV" N.Y. Governor Elliot Lawrence Spitzer #Client9 #FREESILDA

Governor Arnold Schwarzenegger #NannyMildredLoveChild #FREEMARIA

Jailbird U.S. Congressman Anthony David Weiner #Weinergate #FREEHUMA

Alleged Pedophile Woody Allen Teenager Orgies #BelieveBabiChristinaEngelhardt #BelieveDylan

Charlie Rose #TIMESUP

Matthew Todd Lauer #TIMESUP

Jailbird Rapist Harvey Weinstein (50+ Victims) #TIMESUP

Jailbird Rapist Bill Cosby (50+ Victims) #THEEMPTYCHAIR

Jailbird Rapist Larry Nassar (300+ Victims) #USAGYMNASTICS

Bad Boy Sexual Predators:

Jailbird Serial Rapist on N.Y.C. Manhattan's Upper East Side #Castration #Justice

Rapists Drink & Drug College Student Gang-Bangers #Castration #Justice

Rapists Global Sex Traffickers of Women and Children #Castration #Justice

Rapists Spoils of War Sex Slaves #Castration #Justice

Pedophile Catholic Priests of Silly Little Boys #Castration #Justice

©2019. All Rights Reserved. Creative Genius Sharon Esther Lampert

SILLY LITTLE BOYS: 40 RULES OF MANHOOD

Dedication

November 25: International Day for Elimination of Violence Against Women

#ViolenceAgainstWomensAct   #VAWA

#PenisWallofShame

#2018NobelPrizeLiterature

#TIMESUP   #METOO   #IAMBRAVE

#BringBackOurGirls

#Nadia_Murad   #2018NOBELPRIZE

#BelieveSusanMunsey   #2018CNNHERO

#BelieveTaranaBurke   2017 TIME PERSON OF THE YEAR

#BelieveChessyProut15 - Book:"I Have the Right To"

#BelieveMissAmericaMarilyn1958 - Book:"Miss America By Day"

#BelieveMissWorldLinor1998 - Movie:"Brave Miss World"

#BelieveDrFord   #BelieveAnitaHill   #BelieveMimiBeardsley

#BelieveCaelynnMillerKeyes   Movie:"Hunting Ground"   #BelieveElizabethSmart

#BelieveLadyGaga   Song:"Till It Happens to You"   #BelieveEllenDeGeneres

#FREEHILLARY   #FREESILDA   #FREEHUMA   #FREEMARIA   #FREEMELANIA

#INCEST   #SEXUALHARRASSMENT   #SEXUALASSAULT   #RAPE

#MARITALRAPE   #BelieveLorenaBobbitt   #1993FeministHero   #LorenaRedWagon

#BelieveMe   #WhyIDidntReport   #ITSONUS   #HIMTOO   #BelieveWadeRobson

#LetTheGirlsPlay -   Song: "Suffragettes-Time's Up"

©2019. All Rights Reserved. Creative Genius Sharon Esther Lampert

SILLY LITTLE BOYS: 40 RULES OF MANHOOD

Rule 1

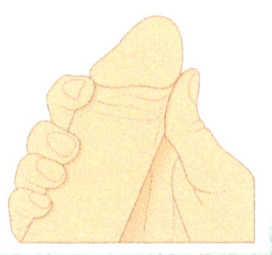

Your PENIS is not a TOY or the CENTER of YOUR ATTENTION!

#SillyLittleBoys

©2019. All Rights Reserved. Creative Genius Sharon Esther Lampert

SILLY LITTLE BOYS: 40 RULES OF MANHOOD

Rule 2

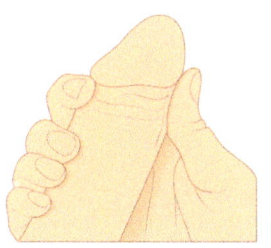

Your PENIS is not the CENTER of HER ATTENTION!

Congratulations to Dyllan McGee for #MakersConference #RaiseYourVoice

©2019. All Rights Reserved. Creative Genius Sharon Esther Lampert

SILLY LITTLE BOYS: 40 RULES OF MANHOOD

Rule 3

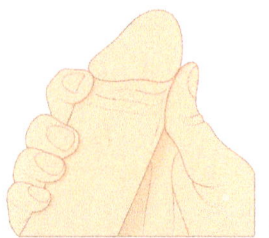

Don't Brag!
Keep Your PENIS
Inside Your Pants!

NO INTERNET/INTRANET PHOTOS!
NO SEXTING! NO DICK PICS!

Don't Be U.S. Congressman Anthony Weiner Jailbird!
#WEINERGATE   #CHILDABUSE   #JAILBIRD   #FREEHUMA

©2019. All Rights Reserved. Creative Genius Sharon Esther Lampert

SILLY LITTLE BOYS: 40 RULES OF MANHOOD

Rule 4

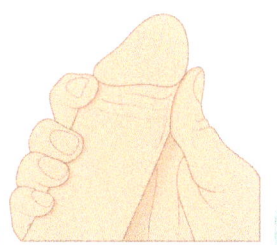

Use Your PENIS to Pee
Focus, Aim, Bullseye
Clean Up Smelly
Urine Splatter!
#BULLSEYE

©2019. All Rights Reserved. Creative Genius Sharon Esther Lampert

SILLY LITTLE BOYS: 40 RULES OF MANHOOD

Rule 5

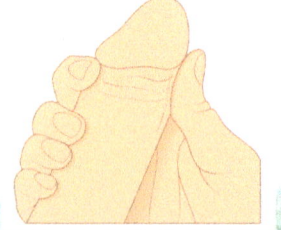

Your Circumcised PENIS
A Medical Procedure and
a Religious Rite of Passage
Paradox: Cut Your Foreskin or Be "Cut Off"
Abraham Covenant (Genesis 17:13)
Those Who Are Not Circumcised Are
"Cut Off" From Their People
[Genesis 17:10–14]

There Is Nothing You Can Do About This!
#GENESIS17:13

©2019. All Rights Reserved. Creative Genius Sharon Esther Lampert

SILLY LITTLE BOYS: 40 RULES OF MANHOOD

Rule 6

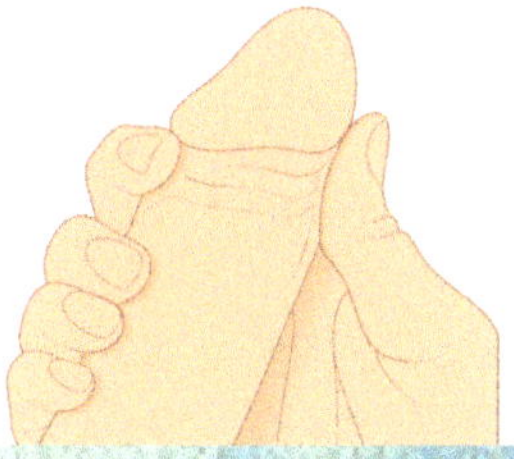

Your Uncircumcised PENIS

You Have a Foreskin
You Have Not Been Mutilated
You Have Extra Nerve Endings
You Have to Clean the "Smegma"
Fatty Oils and Dead Skin Cells
Between Penis and Foreskin
Foreskin Is Good and Bad
Oldest Medical Controversy Ever!

©2019. All Rights Reserved. Creative Genius Sharon Esther Lampert

SILLY LITTLE BOYS: 40 RULES OF MANHOOD

Rule 7

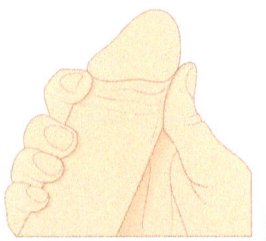

Use Your PENIS to Pleasure Yourself!

#MASTURBATION

©2019. All Rights Reserved. Creative Genius Sharon Esther Lampert

SILLY LITTLE BOYS: 40 RULES OF MANHOOD

Rule 8

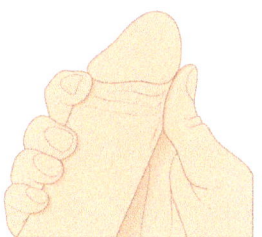

"Perhaps you have figured it out by now, but little girls don't stay little girls forever. They grow into strong women that return to destroy your world!"
#BELIEVE Kyle Stephens
Sexual Abuse: Ages 6-12
Larry Nassar Trial (140 Victims)

Get Permission to Use Your PENIS to Pleasure Another!

Don't Do a Bill Cosby, Larry Nassar or Harvey Weinstein
30 Years to Bring These DICKS to Justice!

#JUSTICE #BetterLateThanNever
#2018NobelPrizeLiterature #SurvivingRKelly #MuteRKelly

©2019. All Rights Reserved. Creative Genius Sharon Esther Lampert

SILLY LITTLE BOYS: 40 RULES OF MANHOOD

Rule 9

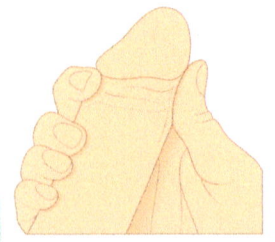

Don't Ask a Girl on a Date
Expecting Sex and the
Instant Gratification
of Your PENIS! (Rule 1)
Just Because She Agreed to
One Thing Doesn't Mean
She Agreed to Everything!

Don't Do Owen Labrie and Lose Your 4-Year Scholarship to Harvard
University Divinity School and Get Listed as a Sex Offender

#BelieveChessyProut15

©2019. All Rights Reserved. Creative Genius Sharon Esther Lampert

SILLY LITTLE BOYS: 40 RULES OF MANHOOD

Rule 10

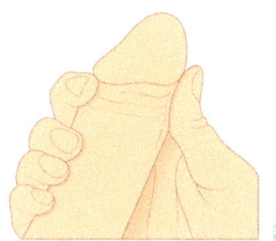

Before You OPEN Your Pants to Show a Girl Your PENIS OPEN Your HEART, OPEN Your MIND, and OPEN Your WALLET

Is Anybody Home?
Be Warm, Loving & Generous

#RESPECT

©2019. All Rights Reserved. Creative Genius Sharon Esther Lampert

SILLY LITTLE BOYS: 40 RULES OF MANHOOD

Rule 11

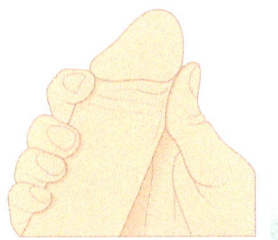

If You Want a Woman to Pay _{double entendre} Attention to Your PENIS:
Don't Expect Sexual Freebies!
Never Arrive Empty Handed!

Gifts: Flowers, Chocolate, Jewelry, Lingerie, Tickets, Travel, Engagement Ring, Cash, Check, Credit Card, Fix Something, Cook a Meal, Do Dishes, Do Laundry, Change Diaper, Walk Dog, Change Cat Litter, Empty Garbage, Help Kids with Homework.

#AlloftheAbove!

©2019. All Rights Reserved. Creative Genius Sharon Esther Lampert

SILLY LITTLE BOYS: 40 RULES OF MANHOOD

Rule 12

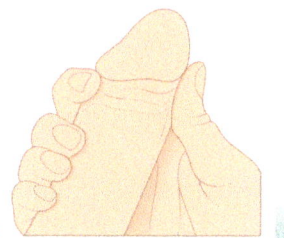

Don't Be a Dick!

"Sex First Love Maybe Marriage Never!"

Sharon Esther Lampert
Poet, Philosopher, Peacemaker, Prophet, Prodigy

#PRICK   #COCK   #DONG   #WONG   #PECKER

©2019. All Rights Reserved. Creative Genius Sharon Esther Lampert

SILLY LITTLE BOYS: 40 RULES OF MANHOOD

Rule 13

Holy Trinity 1
PENIS, PUSSY, AND PLAN

Plan A. One-Night Stand
Plan B. Love Affair
Plan C. Playing the Field
Plan D. Flavor of the Month
Plan E. No Strings Attached: "Fuck Buddy or Friend w/Benefits"
Plan F. Artist and Muse (Immortality!)
Plan G. Boyfriend and Girlfriend
Plan H. Marriage: Husband and Wife (Kids, Pets, Relatives)
Plan I. Rare 1% Unconditional True Love (Best Friends)
Plan J. Pimp and Prostitute: Oldest Profession in the World (Legal and Illegal)
Plan K. Adultery: Lose Almost Everything!

#PenisWallofShame

©2019. All Rights Reserved. Creative Genius Sharon Esther Lampert

SILLY LITTLE BOYS: 40 RULES OF MANHOOD

Rule 14

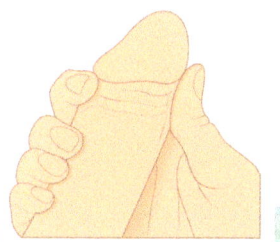

Holy Trinity 2
PENIS, PUSSY, AND LOVE

1. True Love Is Unconditional and Rare 1%
2. Happy Couples Married Their Best Friends
3. STOP Using Pronoun "I" — Only Use "WE"
4. 99% Adult Love Is Conditional Love

Adult Love Is Hard Work and Has Expiration Dates:
Infidelity, Break-Ups, Divorce, Death, and Murder

#HORNDOGJeffBezos   #XRatedDickPics   #Mistress

©2019. All Rights Reserved. Creative Genius Sharon Esther Lampert

SILLY LITTLE BOYS: 40 RULES OF MANHOOD

Rule 15

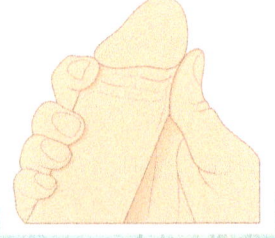

Holy Trinity 3
PENIS, HEART, MIND

When Your 1. PENIS 2. HEART and 3. MIND
All Agree on the Right Mate
Ejaculation Is Ecstasy!

Use Your Penis to #MAKE LOVE

Don't Do a President John F. Kennedy, and Tell Your Mistress Mimi Beardsley to Suck on Your Friend's (and Brother's) Penis Too!

50-Years Later a Book: "I'm Not a Secret Anymore!" #BELIEVE Mimi Beardsley

©2019. All Rights Reserved. Creative Genius Sharon Esther Lampert

SILLY LITTLE BOYS: 40 RULES OF MANHOOD

Rule 16

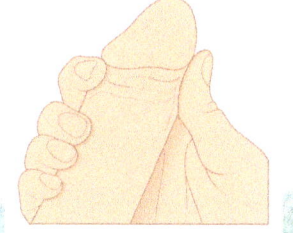

Holy Trinity 4
HAPPY WIFE = HAPPY LIFE

1. A Happy Wife Is a Happy Life!
2. She Is Always Right!
3. Don't Be a Sore Loser: "CUNT!"
4. Make LOVE Not WAR!
5. VAGINA Knows Best!

Don't Do a Dirt-Bag Trump: "Fat" "Pig" "Dog" "Slob" "Disgusting" Animal."

©2019. All Rights Reserved. Creative Genius Sharon Esther Lampert

SILLY LITTLE BOYS: 40 RULES OF MANHOOD

Rule 17

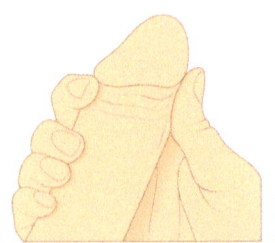

Keep Your BILLIONS of PENIS Sperm on Tight Leashes! Do Not Bring Unwanted and Unloved Children into the World!

Don't Do a Governor Arnold Schwarzenegger Love Child
Don't Impregnate Your Wife and Nanny at the Same Time!

#INFIDELITY   #LOVECHILD   #FREEMARIA

©2019. All Rights Reserved. Creative Genius Sharon Esther Lampert

SILLY LITTLE BOYS: 40 RULES OF MANHOOD

Rule 18

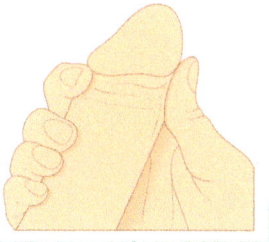

No-Brainer
- Ejaculation does not involve the brain.
- The signal to ejaculate comes from the spinal ejaculation generator in the spinal cord.
- Most men have very little control over exactly when they ejaculate.

You Can Break Your Penis
- There is no bone in your penis—but it is still possible to break your penis.
- Penile fracture is the rupture of the fibrous covering of the corpora cavernosa, the tissue that becomes erect when engorged with blood.
- The most dangerous sexual position is "woman-on-top."

The Size of Your PENIS Matters Only If You Are a Sex Worker Porn Star!

Average Size Erect 5-7 Inches

#JOYSTICK

©2019. All Rights Reserved. Creative Genius Sharon Esther Lampert

SILLY LITTLE BOYS: 40 RULES OF MANHOOD

Rule 19

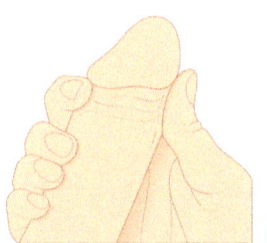

"A man needs to learn how to MAKE LOVE to a women, instead of pissing into her vagina like another toilet bowl."

Sharon Esther Lampert

**During Sex and Love
Be a Gentleman
Let Your Lover
Climax and Orgasm
Before Your PENIS Ejaculates!**
Take Charge of Cleanup
and Do the Laundry!
#GENTLEMAN

©2019. All Rights Reserved. Creative Genius Sharon Esther Lampert

SILLY LITTLE BOYS: 40 RULES OF MANHOOD

Rule 20

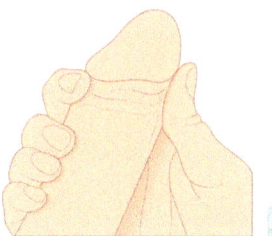

SEXUAL FANTASY

The Operating Manual for Your PENIS is in Your Mind. Your PENIS is a Follower Not a Leader!

#SexualFantasy

©2019. All Rights Reserved. Creative Genius Sharon Esther Lampert

SILLY LITTLE BOYS: 40 RULES OF MANHOOD

Rule 21

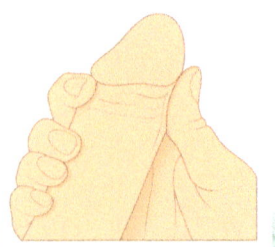

PENIS THERAPY SESSION

The Woman (VAGINA) of Your Sexual Fantasy is NOT the Woman (VAGINA) You Want to Marry and Raise Your Kids!

#LUST

©2019. All Rights Reserved. Creative Genius Sharon Esther Lampert

SILLY LITTLE BOYS: 40 RULES OF MANHOOD

Rule 22

"Human Rights Are Women's Rights! And Women's Rights Are Human Rights!"
— Hillary Rodham Clinton

MINUS ZERO WOMAN
A Women Is Raised to Believe That Without a Man, She Is NOTHING!. Only to Find Out That With a Man; SHE IS LESS THAN NOTHING!
— Sharon Esther Lampert

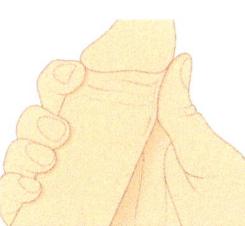

Vaginas Run the World

Without a VAGINA, You Cease to Exist! Women Have the Power to Abort a Male Fetus and Terminate Men! #ABORTION You Should Bow Down and Worship the VAGINA Like a #GOD!

Sharon Esther Lampert
Poet, Philosopher, Peacemaker, Prophet, Prodigy

#14THAmmendment1868 #19THAmmendent1920 #ERA1921-1982
#ROEVSWADE1973

©2019. All Rights Reserved. Creative Genius Sharon Esther Lampert

SILLY LITTLE BOYS: 40 RULES OF MANHOOD

SHUT IT DOWN!
PORNHUB.COM
- Child Rapes
- Revenge Pornography
- Spy Cams of Women Showering
- Racist and Misogynist Content
- Women Asphyxiated in Plastic Bags
- 3.5 Billion Visits a Week (#1 Website)

Poisonous-Snake Psychopaths are problems of NATURE: "Snatch, Seize, and Destroy!"

Rule 23

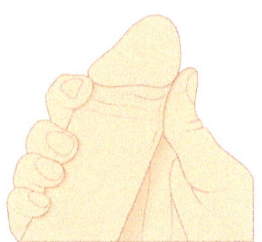

"BE HARD ON A WOMAN ONLY WHEN MAKING LOVE TO HER!"

Sharon Esther Lampert
Poet, Philosopher, Peacemaker, Prophet, Prodigy

#Believe Miss Israel—Miss World Linor Abargil
Violent Rape Two Months Before Miss World Beauty Pageant 1998
Watch Her Movie, "BRAVE MISS WORLD"
#IAMBRAVE

©2019. All Rights Reserved. Creative Genius Sharon Esther Lampert

SILLY LITTLE BOYS: 40 RULES OF MANHOOD

Rule 24

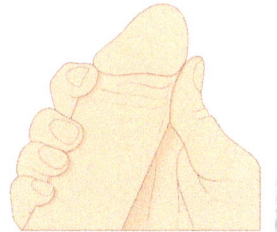

TWO KINDS of MEN (PENIS)

"There Are Only Two Kinds of Men (PENIS) in This World The BIG DICKS Who Know How to Build Something and the small dicks Who Know How to Destroy Everything!"

Sharon Esther Lampert
Poet, Philosopher, Peacemaker, Prophet, Prodigy

#BIGDICKS   #smalldicks

©2019. All Rights Reserved. Creative Genius Sharon Esther Lampert

SILLY LITTLE BOYS: 40 RULES OF MANHOOD

Rule 25

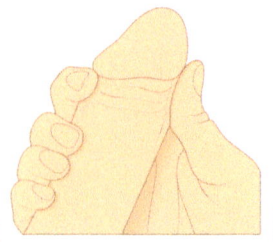

THE PENIS PARADOX

Why Is it that the Men with No Dicks Are the Men Who Become the Dicks?

Sharon Esther Lampert
Poet, Philosopher, Peacemaker, Prophet, Prodigy

#PENISPARADOX

©2019. All Rights Reserved. Creative Genius Sharon Esther Lampert

SILLY LITTLE BOYS: 40 RULES OF MANHOOD

Rule 26

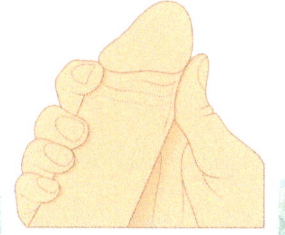

Use Your PENIS to Become a Sperm Donor and Help Infertile Couples. You Must Be a College Graduate.
(Pay Off College Loans)

#PENISCASHCOW   #SPERMDONER

©2019. All Rights Reserved. Creative Genius Sharon Esther Lampert

SILLY LITTLE BOYS: 40 RULES OF MANHOOD

Rule 27

Don't Do a Roman Polanski
#BELIEVE Samantha Geimer
Drugged and Raped at 13

Don't Do a Woody Allen
Amazon cancels Woody Allen's 4-film contract, and the release of his movie, "Rainy Day in New York!" (Poetic Justice)
#BELIEVE DylanFarrow1992

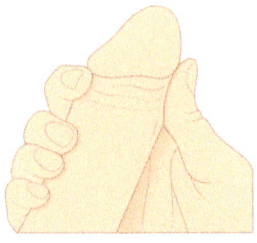

WARNING!
In prison, sex offenders and child molesters are the lowest of the low among criminals.

Penis Global Catastrophe #1
STOP Sticking Your PENIS Into Your Daughter's VAGINA!

GET HELP ASAP!

#INCEST   #MOLESTATION

#BelieveMissAmericaMarilyn   #BelieveRitaHayworth
#BelieveEveEnsler   #BelieveSandreDee   #BelieveRoseanneBarr
#BelieveDylanFarrow   #BelieveLisaYvonneFrench

Oprah's Child Predator Watch List: $100,000 Reward
#Believe Oprah Winfrey, Pregnant at Age 13

©2019. All Rights Reserved. Creative Genius Sharon Esther Lampert

SILLY LITTLE BOYS: 40 RULES OF MANHOOD

Rule 28

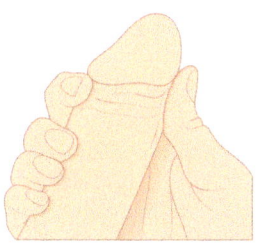

WARNING
40 Million People Worldwide (Mayo Clinic)
AIDS: Acquired Immunodeficiency Syndrome
HIV: Human Immunodeficiency Virus

Penis Global Catastrophe #2

"LOVE HURTS! HIV/AIDS KILLS! CONDOMS RULE! LONG LIVE SAFE SEX!"

Sharon Esther Lampert
Poet, Philosopher, Peacemaker, Prophet, Prodigy

#STEALTHING
Removal of a Condom
During Sexual Intercourse
without Consent is a Crime
Canada, Switzerland, Germany

Don't Do Jailbird Philippe Padieu
Who Gave 6 Women AIDS
Assault with Deadly Weapon,
His Bodily Fluid
#OPRAHWINFREYSHOW

©2019. All Rights Reserved. Creative Genius Sharon Esther Lampert

SILLY LITTLE BOYS: 40 RULES OF MANHOOD

Rule 29

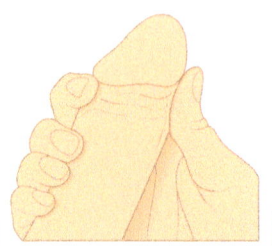

WARNING!
RAPE: Usually Someone You Know!
75%: Father, relative, teacher, neighbor, doctor, boss, professor, date, fiance, or husband.
25%: Pervert hiding in bushes.

Penis Global Catastrophe #3
STOP Bragging! SEX IS NOT A SPORT!
STOP Counting PENIS Penetrations and Ejaculations 1, 2, 3, 4, 5... 100+

SEXUAL CONQUESTS and SHAMING WOMEN #SLUT
Don't Make You a Man!
You Have Become a Sexual Predator!

Get Help ASAP!

#PenisOutofControl   #OutofControlPenis

©2019. All Rights Reserved. Creative Genius Sharon Esther Lampert

SILLY LITTLE BOYS: 40 RULES OF MANHOOD

Rule 30

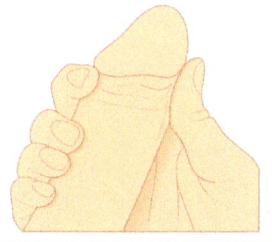

Penis Global Catastrophe #4

PENIS ABUSE!
STOP Wasting Your Time (Rule 1) Masturbating to Online Flawless Photoshopped Fake Women! You Will Become Addicted to Internet Pornography!

Get Help ASAP!

©2019. All Rights Reserved. Creative Genius Sharon Esther Lampert

SILLY LITTLE BOYS: 40 RULES OF MANHOOD

CONGRATULATIONS!
2017 TIME Person of the Year!
Founder Tarana Burke
ME TOO! MOVEMENT
#Believe Tarana Burke

Rule 31

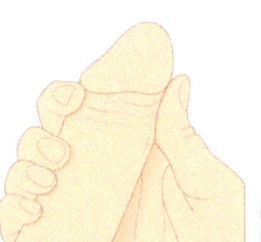

WE WANT JUSTICE!
"And when you're a star, they let you do it. **You can do anything! Grab 'em by the pussy! You can do anything!**" (U-Tube)
US President Donald Trump
Self-Proclaimed Pussy Grabber

Penis Global Catastrophe #5
If You Are Happy or Unhappily Married, **STOP** Sexual Harassment of PENIS at Work to Coworkers for Extramartial Sex
No Career Advancement for Sex

DON'T BE A CUOMO SEX PEST!
DON'T BE A TRUMP PUSSY GRABBER!

#PUSSYGRABBER   #FREEMELANIA   #BEBEST

#BELIEVEStormy   #BELIEVEKaren   #BELIEVEJessica   #BELIEVEKristin   #BELIEVECathy
#BELIEVETemple   #BELIEVEKarena   #BELIEVEMindy   #BELIEVERachel   #BELIEVENatasha
#BELIEVEJuliet   #BELIEVEJessica   #BELIEVEMissFinlandNinni   #BELIEVECassandra

#LillyLedbetterFairPayAct2009

©2019. All Rights Reserved. Creative Genius Sharon Esther Lampert

SILLY LITTLE BOYS: 40 RULES OF MANHOOD

"First We Cry Then We Fight"
#Believe Gloria Allred

Rule 32

2020: CUOMOSEXUALS
2021: CUOMO SEX PEST

#Believe 11 Women
- Executive Assistant #1 - Grouped
- Trooper #1
- Charlotte Bennett
- Lindsey Boylan
- Alyssa McGrath
- Ana Liss
- Kaitlin
- State Entity Employee #1 - Grouped
- State Entity Employee #2
- Virginia Limmiatis - Grouped
- Anna Ruch

#Believe Shelley Ross, 2005
Chris Cuomo accused of sexually harassing ex-boss Shelley Ross at party —playfully pitching her buttocks!

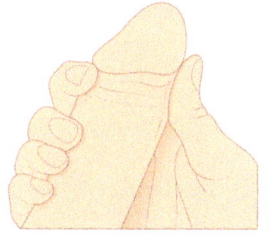

Penis Global Catastrophe #6
Hot Sex Forever!
Married Sex No More!
STOP Sexual Harrassment of Every Woman (VAGINA) Who Crosses Your Path
You Are a Sex Addict!
Get Help ASAP!

Don't Be Impeached President William Jefferson Clinton

#SlickWillie   #FREEHILLARY   #IMWITHHER
#BELIEVEJuanita   #BELIEVEKathleen   #BELIEVEPaula
#BELIEVELeslie   #BELIEVEMonica   #BELIEVEGennifer

©2019. All Rights Reserved. Creative Genius Sharon Esther Lampert

SILLY LITTLE BOYS: 40 RULES OF MANHOOD

Rule 33

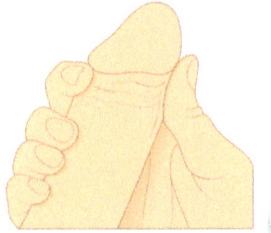

Penis Global Catastrophe #7
GBR UNIVERSITY DEGREE
STOP Inviting Women to a Party to Drink, Drug and Sexually Assault Women! Don't Graduate College with the Degree of GBR "Gang-Banger Rapist!"
This Is Not a School Tradition!
Get Help ASAP! Watch Movie, "Hunting Ground"
#ViolenceAgainstWomenAct1994
Don't Be Alleged Supreme Court Justice "BLACKOUT" Kavanaugh!
#BELIEVE Dr. Ford"   #HuntingGround   #BELIEVE Caelynn Miller Keyes

©2019. All Rights Reserved. Creative Genius Sharon Esther Lampert

SILLY LITTLE BOYS: 40 RULES OF MANHOOD

Rule 34

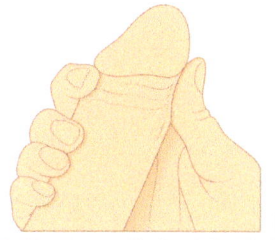

Penis Global Catastrophe #8

Your PENIS Is Not a **Weapon of War** to Rape, Humiliate, and Subjugate!
A Vagina is Not a Spoil of War!

Get Help ASAP! #Castration

#BringBackOurGirls Chibok Girls, Nigeria

Congratulations Nadia Murad on Your 2018 Nobel Peace

©2019. All Rights Reserved. Creative Genius Sharon Esther Lampert

SILLY LITTLE BOYS: 40 RULES OF MANHOOD

2019: Child Rapist, Serial Rapist, and Sex Trafficker
- JEFFREY EPSTEIN (and Madam Ghislaine Maxwell)
- THE LOLITA EXPRESS
- LITTLE JEFF'S ORGY ISLAND
- PRINCE ANDREW STEPS DOWN
- ALAN DERSHOWITZ RANT "YES MASSAGE! NO SEX!"
- Book: "Training With Miss Abernathy: A Workbook for Erotic Slaves and Their Owners"
- Book: "Epstein's Little Black Book"

#BELIEVE Virginia Roberts Giuffre, Jane Doe #3
#BELIEVE Jane Does:
- Alicia Arden
- Sarah Ransome
- Sigrid McCawley
- Courtney Wild
- Michelle Licata
- Johanna Sjoberg
- Annie Farmer

Rule 35

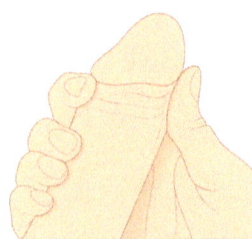

Under 16: Sexual Abuse of Minor (his fault)

Over 16: Professional Sex Worker (her fault)

Penis Global Catastrophe #9

STOP Setting **TRAPS** to Kidnap and Chain Women to Bedposts to Have Sex with 10 Men a Day!

Don't Sell Women (Vaginas) to Sex Traffickers!
A VAGINA IS NOT A CASH COW!
Get Help ASAP! #Castration

Congratulations Susan Munsey on 2018 CNN Hero Award!

©2019. All Rights Reserved. Creative Genius Sharon Esther Lampert

SILLY LITTLE BOYS: 40 RULES OF MANHOOD

December 17, 2019
Historic Vatican Ruling
Pope Francis declared the end of the "Pontifical Secret" for sexual abuse of minors and for Clerics with PORN (age 18).

2018: NUNS JOIN "ME TOO!"
"The Vatican has long been aware of nuns sexually abused by priests and bishops in Asia, Europe, South America and Africa, but it has done very little to stop it." (AP)

Rule 36

February 2019
Profile in Courage
Congratulations Margaret Markey!
Child Victims Act, NY
Criminal charges until a victim turns 28 and assault survivors can file lawsuits until age 55. A one-year "look-back window" to allow expired cases to become newly viable. Law passed after 13 years of activism.

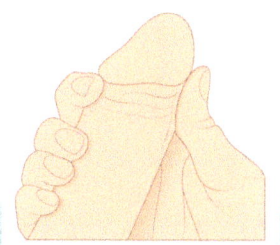

Penis Global Catastrophe #10

Don't Give Your LIFE to JESUS and Your PENIS to the DEVIL
Silly Little Boys Are Victims of Sexual Assault Too!
Catholic Priests Need Mandatory Masturbation Education
#Pedophile Catholic Priests Use
Silly Little Boys for "Cheat Treats!"
And Silly Little Girls (NUNS) for "Cheat Treats!"

Catholic Churches File for Bankruptcy!

Don't Do a Michael Jackson Pedophile "Leaving Neverland"!

#BELIEVE James Safechuck **Get Help ASAP!** #BELIEVE Wade Robson

"500 More Clergy Abuse Cases" Washington Post, Dec. 19, 2018

©2019. All Rights Reserved. Creative Genius Sharon Esther Lampert

SILLY LITTLE BOYS: 40 RULES OF MANHOOD

SHUT IT DOWN!
PORNHUB.COM
- Child Rapes
- Revenge Pornography
- Spy Cams of Women Showering
- Racist and Misogynist Content
- Women Asphyxiated in Plastic Bags.
- 3.5 Billion Visits a Week (#1 Online Site)

Rule 37

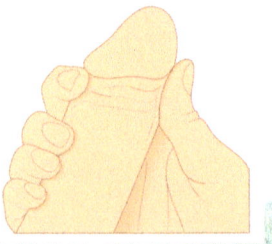

#BELIEVE Elizabeth Smart, Age 14, Utah, USA Abducted inside her home in the middle of the night and held captive for 9 months. Raped multiple times a day!
#CASTRATION #VAWA

Penis National Catastrophe #11
SEXUALLY EXPLOITED CHILDREN
Don't Take Your PENIS on a Trip to CAMBODIA
To Have Sex with a Child!
Don't Pack Barbie Dolls as Gifts!
One-Third of Sex-Trafficking Victims in
Prostitution are Children Under Age 15!

Get Help ASAP! #CASTRATION

Don't Do a Dr. Clive Robert Cressy

**Congratulations Ashton Kutcher and Demi Moore on
THORN: Digital Defenders of Sexually Exploited Children**

©2019. All Rights Reserved. Creative Genius Sharon Esther Lampert

SILLY LITTLE BOYS: 40 RULES OF MANHOOD

Rule 38

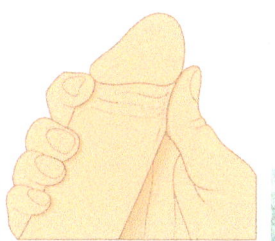

WARNING! In prison, sex offenders and child molestors are the lowest of the low among criminals.

Penis National Catastrophe #12

INFANT RAPES
Don't Rape African Infant Girls to "Cure" Your AIDS Infection!

Get Help ASAP! #CASTRATION

Congratulations Dr. Denis Mukwege on Your 2018 Nobel Peace

©2019. All Rights Reserved. Creative Genius Sharon Esther Lampert

SILLY LITTLE BOYS: 40 RULES OF MANHOOD

Rule 39

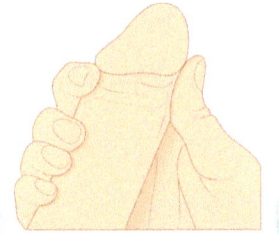

Penis Global Catastrophe #13
#RICHLIMPPIMP

You Are a Rich Old Man
Your PENIS Is a Limp Dick!
You Will Use VIAGRA to Extend the
Life of Your PENIS
(You Will Move to Florida)
STOP Sexually Harrassing
Young Babes on a Limp Dick!
Help Is on the Way! Rule 40!

©2019. All Rights Reserved. Creative Genius Sharon Esther Lampert

SILLY LITTLE BOYS: 40 RULES OF MANHOOD

Rule 40

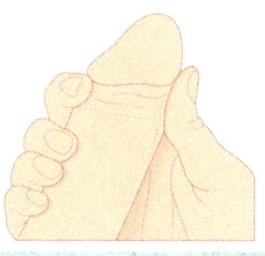

#BELIEVE Kemal's Mother
Morgue Rapist: David Fuller
Azra Kemal's body was raped three times in July 2020 in the morgue of Tunbridge Wells hospital by David Fuller, a hospital electrician who is known to have violated at least 100 corpses between 2008 and 2010. The sentence for necrophilia is two years in jail.

Penis Global Catastrophe #14

When You Are a Demented Old Man with a Limp Dick in a Nursing Home

STOP USING VIAGRA

STOP Sexually Harrassing the HELP!
Young Babe Nurses and Old Broad Nurses
Don't Die a Sexual Predator on the Internet

#PENISWallofShame

©2019. All Rights Reserved. Creative Genius Sharon Esther Lampert

SILLY LITTLE BOYS: 40 RULES OF MANHOOD

SEE THE WORLD THROUGH THE EYES OF A CREATIVE GENIUS
SHARON ESTHER LAMPERT

Poet
Philosopher
Peacemaker
Prophet
Paladin of Education
Photon Superhero
Pin-Up
Princess Kadimah
Phoenix
Prodigy

©2019. All Rights Reserved. Creative Genius Sharon Esther Lampert

SILLY LITTLE BOYS: 40 RULES OF MANHOOD

ALSO BY THE CREATIVE GENIUS
SHARON ESTHER LAMPERT

Contributions to Civilization

POETRY
The Greatest Poems Ever Written on Extraordinary World Events

PHILOSOPHY
40 Absolute Truths of Natural Philosophy

CREATIVITY
10 Esoteric Laws of Genius and Creativity

EDUCATION
SMARTGRADES BRAIN POWER REVOLUTION

LOVE
CUPID: WRITTEN IN LETTER C

THEOLOGY
GOD IS GO! DO!
GOD TALKS TO ME
22 COMMANDMENTS

WORLD PEACE
The World Peace Equation
SILLY LITTLE BOYS: 40 RULES OF MANHOOD

©2019. All Rights Reserved. Creative Genius Sharon Esther Lampert

SEE THE WORLD THROUGH THE EYES OF A CREATIVE GENIUS

www.SharonEstherLampert.com

POET
"A" Listed as One of the World's Greatest Poets
The Greatest Poems Ever Written on Extraordinary World Events
www.WorldFamousPoems.com

CUPID—Written in Letter C

PHILOSOPHER
GOD OF WHAT? Is Life a Gift or a Punishment?
www.PhilosopherQueen.com

PROPHET
GOD TALKS TO ME: A WORKING DEFINITION OF GOD
THE 22 COMMANDMENTS: All You Will Ever Need to Know About God

PEACEMAKER
WORLD PEACE EQUATION

PALADIN OF EDUCATION
SMARTGRADES BRAIN POWER REVOLUTION
www.SMARTGRADEScom

PRODIGY
UNLEASH THE GOD WITHIN: 10 Esoteric Laws of Genius and Creativity
www.SharonEstherLampert.com

POPULAR
"SCHMALTZY: IN AMERICA EVEN A CAT CAN HAVE A DREAM"
First Book of Color Coded Vocabulary Words to Help Kids Learn
www.Schmaltzy.com

SEX ON A PLATE: FOOD AS FOREPLAY
The Coobook of Everlasting Love
www.TrueLoveBurnsEternal.com

November 25: International Day for the Elimination of Violence Against Women

16+ Global Castastrophes of Violence Against Women

1. Incest: Sex with Your Own Children
2. AIDS
3. Sport of Sexual Predation & Slut Shaming
4. Addiction to Pornography & Crime of Child Pornography
5. SEX PESTS: Sexual Harassment at Work
6. PUSSY GRABBERS: Hot Sex Forever; Married Sex No More!
7. Gang-Banger Drug & Rape of University Students
8. Weapons of War Rapists
9. Global Sex Traffickers of Women & Prostitution
10. Church Pedophiles Sexually Assaulting Boys & Nuns Too!
11. Cambodia: Sex Traffickers of Children & Prostitution
12. Africa: Raping Infants to Cure AIDS
13. RICH LIMP PIMPS
14. Nursing Home Harassment of Women Staff
+ 15. India: Forced Marriage of Daughter for Money (YouTube)
+ 16. Bulgaria: Selling Daughters into Marriage (YouTube)

FAIR USE NOTICE

This book contains material which may not have been authorized by the copyright owners. We are making such material available in our efforts to advance understanding of social justice, political, human rights and democracy issues. We believe this constitutes a 'fair use' of any such copyrighted material as provided for in section 107 of the US Copyright Law.

www.ingramcontent.com/pod-product-compliance
Lightning Source LLC
Chambersburg PA
CBHW041217240426
43661CB00012B/1071